AS FAR AS YOU KNOW

ALSO BY A. F. MORITZ

Poetry

Here
Black Orchid
Between the Root and the Flower
The Visitation
The Tradition
Song of Fear
The Ruined Cottage
Ciudad interior
Phantoms in the Ark
Mahoning
Houseboat on the Styx
Rest on the Flight into Egypt
The End of the Age
Conflicting Desire
Early Poems
Night Street Repairs
The Sentinel
The New Measures
Sequence
The Sparrow: Selected Poems

As Editor

The Best Canadian Poetry in English, 2009
The 2010 Griffin Poetry Prize Anthology

Translation

Children of the Quadrilateral: Selected Poetry of Benjamin Péret
Testament for Man: Selected Poems of Gilberto Meza

Translation of Works by Ludwig Zeller

Ludwig Zeller in the Country of the Antipodes: Poems 1964–1979
The Marble Head and Other Poems
The Ghost's Tattoos
Body of Insomnia and Other Poems
Rio Loa: Station of Dreams
Woman in Dream
The Rules of the Game: Selected Shorter Poems 1952–2008
For a Savage Love: Three Books

AS FAR AS YOU KNOW

POEMS

A. F. Moritz

ANANSI

Published in Canada in 2020 and the USA in 2020 by House of Anansi Press Inc.
www.houseofanansi.com

House of Anansi Press is committed to protecting our natural environment. As part of our efforts, the interior of this book is printed on paper that is made from second-growth forests and is acid-free.

24 23 22 21 20 1 2 3 4 5

Library and Archives Canada Cataloguing in Publication
Title: As far as you know / A. F. Moritz.
Names: Moritz, A. F. (Albert Frank), author.
Description: Poems.
Identifiers: Canadiana (print) 2019017241X | Canadiana (ebook) 20190172428 | ISBN 9781487007409 (softcover) | ISBN 9781487007423 (hardcover) | ISBN 9781487007416 (PDF)
Classification: LCC PS8576.O724 A82 2020 | DDC C811/.54—dc23

Cover design: Alysia Shewchuk
Cover artwork: Mara Korkola, from *No place 367*
Typesetting: Sara Loos

Canada Council for the Arts / Conseil des Arts du Canada
ONTARIO ARTS COUNCIL / CONSEIL DES ARTS DE L'ONTARIO
an Ontario government agency / un organisme du gouvernement de l'Ontario

We acknowledge for their financial support of our publishing program the Canada Council for the Arts, the Ontario Arts Council, and the Government of Canada.

Printed and bound in Canada

And the form of every single grain will be restored in glory.
I was judged because I was unable to understand this.
— Czesław Miłosz

These tears fall for the little ones...
Lest they be annihilated in thy annihilation.
— William Blake

CONTENTS

Terrorism

Poetry

Childhood Friends

The One Who Answers the Call

TERRORISM

Terrorism

Grackles and starlings
take the fountain:
                                        an October bath
                                        a ceaseless
while it lasts
                            coming
going
              and coming

One terminus of their flurry: the wide bowl
and its twenty standing crystal
cords
            each one emerging as a stalk
rising
              the drops
separating
                        now a necklace of diamonds
with no thread except direction: still
                                                                  upward
and no curve
                              until wait!
                                                the lightness
of weight
                        gives a new motive
down

The water at the highest
                                                limit reaches
the moment
to halt
                spread

become
something else
now
a chalice a smooth
flower a kiss
to the sky and next
the return
showering down
into the pool
to absorb
and begin

The other term of the happy flights
this day is many terms
all the crowns and needle castles
of the near trees
an Austrian pine
a red oak
a green ash
a northern catalpa
scabbards and blades waiting to fall
to the hands of child musketeers
long brown seed pods
up in the floating
mountain of leaves
that shine with the hue
of grass in early April

On a limb
among the five- and seven-fingered leaves
of the ash
one grackle
wet from the bath
stops and stays

to scratch behind its ear
sudden feathered cat
before fluttering back
to the other bird-children at the basin
pausing playing
going coming
from shadowy rests
to the light water

*

Into the space between two trees
a jetliner
emerges perfectly
silent
faraway
needle of light
drawing no thread

So slow
serene
univocal its flight
passing across the pure blue interval

Yet poor I expect
to see it fall from the sky

A globed flash
a star murdered in an instant

And I would find myself
thinking as if unconcerned
of the many
who died there

just now
in a blink of light
so far away
engulfed
in the day's bright quiet

and the human bodies
ashes
fragments
too distant to be distinguished
sifting down
through the air in the remote
catastrophe
to me only a sudden
wink of change
like a glint off dew
almost lost in the brilliant
background
immense
the huge sky
beyond me everywhere
and the raucous
(but stilled by the vastness)
peace here
the birds' and mine

*

It sparkles
the jetliner
it shines
and the starlings
dark glinting
don't notice it

but I fear
and would hate a still
and empty sky

Dread now
lives and pollutes
in the birds' oblivious world
my dread

of the living emptiness like the sky
the days after Pearl Harbor
that Robinson Jeffers in his poem wrote
into the record
of the permanent
facts of earth:

"cleared...
the sky of planes, the windows of light:
these clearings
/
Make a great beauty...
Darkness
and silence,
the two eyes
that see God"

The great
poet meant of course
that the dark and the still
are not eyes
and nothing
is in them
seen

In the earth's permanent facts the sky
is always empty
of its airy navies
its commerce
and is always silent
as on the first morning
and that other first morning
the last the immediate
aftermath
of self
annihilation

Always there
is
in the sky
the erasure of the human
and the sky's regathered
silence
identical
with the silence before the human
the one same
absence
now and always
there in the sky

*

The silver bird on high
passing east
in its landing approach
has buried
or hidden itself
in the tip of a tree
and the noise of the city

arises
        and fills the dome

                    The silence
does not always appear to us
but we have seen it

                We saw the silent sky
of Pearl Harbor again
at the heart of the world
on nine eleven and after
                    That moment of the sky
abandoned by man
                forbidden to us
feared
        how desolate it was
                    That desolation
was to be
the last man
and to walk under

                the emptiness
We were all given the heart then
of some great
            ignored
                disappointed
poet who can project
life into nonentity: we saw
ourselves walking on earth
in our own death
                after our death
the death of us all
                we met
in a fountain-centred garden

the beautiful earth
we had made and we walked
through our own deserted works
ruins still almost new
gardens recently tended
where no one ever comes now
not even ourselves
yet we are there our own ghosts
our own absence and we walk
in stunned admiring dread
among the flowers and birds
that continue to joy in
what humans made
not even noticing the absence
of the gardeners
the builders
                        But now
it all begins imperceptibly
to fall apart because those workers
never will return
to weed to repair
                                    And we
who joyed in those paths among the
grackles and lilies
are not
                are no longer
are only there
to see ourselves
not there

                    (Remember
the birds at Shiloh
                                    who went on singing
in the all-dominant

bombardment
                    went on fluttering chirping
and occasionally one of them fell dead
meeting by chance a musket ball
in the air among the trees from which every leaf
had already been shot away)

*

Another jet
                appears like the last one
in the space between
                    the same green crown
and green-gold tower
                    it sparkles the same
in the unanimous blue
between the catalpa
                    and the maidenhair
following the same
                    glide path down
drawing its
                invisible threads
passengers
lives
along above the ceaseless
                        moment of the birds'

and the waters'

and my

happiness

October 2012

POETRY

The Ram

The powerful animal with its strange curled horns:
what was left of its heart after the man and boy
appeared, came near, and then the flare of violence,
the man crying, seizing the boy who had walked
ahead of him steadily—the man forcing him down
across the flat rock, golden and pink in the light
that still touched that peak from the western sun—
the boy's back bent across the rock's faint curvature,
his belly bowed upward, his mouth, at first,
screaming? The other one bound him, stripped him, crying,
then fell to his knees, back turned to the rock,
still not seeing the great animal caught in the brambles.

The powerful animal with its strange curled horns.
Wild sheep, age-old emblem of lust and power
and music. Curled horns like giant shells
that are like the curls of breakers that are like
whirlwinds of white dust cut by spiralling dark bands.
It had quit struggling, worn out, before they came
and then had thrashed a little at their approach
and then had stilled again, watching the conflict.

Its eye was vast, some gluey greyness in the corners
but filled almost entirely with the iris's
perfect circle of bright gold, slit top to bottom
with a thin vertical of parabolic blackness
sharpened to points at the vertices.
Its look might have been demonic, mild, or blank,
the horns withheld their shock off other horns
that carried across deep valleys on afternoons
of crystal. Crystal glinted in the rocks, formed

in the pressure of those cliffs. The muscles rested,
the muzzle panted, the sides rose and fell in their coat,
their gleaming blanket, a dreaming child's. Unreadable
its rhythm: calm motions, elements of stillness.
Not sayable by any tongue but its own body.
A foreign word that no one could translate,
therefore inserted whole, not understood and so
passed over a long while, into the muttering, snivelling,
howling distorted text—speech or prayer—of the man
and his long quietening sobs.

The air, the boy's white
body, beautiful, wormlike, the cold black place
in long and longer shadows, the powerful animal
with its curled horns, emblem of lust, power,
music, of the year's birth: of the seizing of dreary space,
new action in the light, greening of delicious grass
in high meadows, the fresh gust of spring—
the seizure of eminence, dominance: the powerful
animal lay mild and watchful, maybe accepting,
maybe worn out, when the man with his knife, his head
full of mucus and salt, turned and across the boy's
almost breaking spine, thrust-up sex and belly, saw.

October 2013

A Book Travels

A book travels through the world,
a closed coffer: a box of jewels,
or a tiny casket in which someone carries in her lap
the body, the ash, of the best beloved.
If it opens, the sun rises,
a paper star springing from the pages
of a child's pop-up book, enclosing
the nuclear fire as it used to burn
in Trebisond. It gleams over a world
of farms and forests. The face of the reader
leans closer, enormous sunflower
above the sun, far above the plain of people
no larger than the letters in a book. From dawn
to sunset and on through night
it turns following its earth.

mid-October 2013

A Throw of the Dice

A throw of the dice will never abolish chance.
But it does. You make your play and there it lies:
a six. You lose. You lose this time forever.
Chance is gone, replaced by fate, your destiny
of stone. But you can pick them up again. Those bones.
Unabolished, chance makes its return.
A phoenix from ashes, a mummy from the tomb,
soaring above, striking terror all through
what had obliterated it. Take courage. Throw.
You duck your head in prayer. For now,
this while, on the verge, there exists even luck.
Good luck, bad luck: some kind of knack
for attracting disaster or averting it.
Now you've unfrozen, the cubes roll again,
and this time: seven spots, or twelve. You win.
And everything's back at rest. Everything always
comes back to rest, in fortune or despair:
the way it is now, the only way things are.
How can this deep freeze enclose
and ever come to sprout freedom and fear?
You are the only ice, the only stake,
the only dice. Every throw was one throw
or it still is: in the closed or open parlour,
you are the mirror or the window.

3 September 2014

Troubadour

Better if I'd been a wandering song
and now were its memory—
words that mixed once in the clear
scent of the river, dissolved and went along,
a cooler freshness in the current.
The story of the disaster
of some great knight and lady
imprisoned in illusion,
the rhymes falling like rain, like glistening
darts and lustres of the dust or snow
in the sun of summer or winter...

Better if I had been the ballad
and now were the memory of it—how good it was,
now utterly forgotten: no knowledge
remains except that it was perfect
beauty in pain, was perfect pleasure. Better
no singer of it ever existed and so
no stumbling singer now survives
with folds of neck sagging to the ground,
its witness and its refutation.

22 February 2015

How You Love, How You Think

Where are the birds
unseen
gabbling and astir
in leaves
that hang unmoving
here where the wind
is dead
a body gone
into the blaze
of air
vibrating

Then eruption:
the birds come gliding
from their hidden places
down slides of air
to the fountain's pool
to play there
to drink to live
to bathe and repair
feathers for flight

Then night comes
the garden now grey
a concert of greys
of bodies given back
to the dissolving
of the limits
the body's vague loom that was

invisible in the clarity
of the cut stone
of noon

The sun has given way
to three thousand suns
the power of the visible
too far off
to warm you
How you love the fear of death
and sorrow of the dead
in the night garden
How you think of them
in peace
and feel a companion
in the night garden
everlasting memory
a hand on your shoulder
that is a breath
of the breathless stillness

You breathe
I wish
this night
would never end

Where are the birds
they're somewhere here
black engravings
on black slate
three or four bodies

barely breathing
along a branch
barely made out
its tree lost
in the black noplace
in the mind imagining—
three or four
children sunk
together
apart
in the intense comfort
of sleep.

4–5 March 2015

As Far As You Know

When you last saw me I was waiting
and now that you will never see me again
for all you know I still am. The time
it turned out was the last time I was sitting
staring across the top edge of the book
into something just above and past
the poem you couldn't see there on the page
between us. Or I was walking—many times
you saw me walking and I can't know
if once when you glimpsed me far away
in the park, too far away to hail,
and you thought you'd tell me later,
it would be fun to laugh over, that almost
meeting in one of the places that are ours
was the last time. Maybe I was lying
suspiciously tired-seeming, my eyes to the ceiling.
When you last saw me I was waiting
like you for us to meet. And now
I still am, as far as you know.

12 April 2015

Further Nudity

She lay there smiling as I took
her clothes off because she knew
when she was naked she would still
be covered. "Women—the self-
fig-leafed," she laughed, happy
that there was more to bare.
We looked into those valleys,
we spread those frills, and sometimes
the small doors there
grew wide enough that the first
edge of the inner darkness could be seen
peeking back—a beautiful naked
householder fearfully calmly
opening to the expected stranger.

16 April 2015

Naked to All Interpretation

There is a speaking in tongues by the dead,
like the anaesthetic babble
of a patient held down in death-likeness by his drugs:
geyser of vituperation and sentiment, names
of lost dogs and lovers—faces
melting together in a fire. And what is mixed there…
the listeners, pausing with sponge, clamp,
bisturi, and laser scalpel, can't make it out.
The voice of the dead through another
head, another voice—a widow
doddering, rocking her body, in the cemetery
where her lover festers. The voice of the dead,
the poem naked to all interpretation,
a muttering humming with no one now
to speak for it. Its author, its husband gone, the one
who raised it from the stony beach of sounds.
Its shepherd gone, leaving it
wandering idly around. A thread stretching
with knots of rage and homesick lamentation
through all ears, mouths, and streets.

29 April 2015

Silence and Song

In paintings a divinity lives,
an aspect and presence of divinity:
the silence. Gratefully the body
drinks it through the eyes.
They see it's a member of the body
beyond the skin—missing member, how long
missed: without it long the body dies.
Quiet water. Empty shelter
waiting, far off across a plain,
like towers, or just a ruined wall,
and the vast early evening that encloses them,
far off and long before the tired traveller, drawing near,
can hear the bees swarm in the lavender fields
and cattle lowing near the falls. Divine
silence of the poem, silence it gathers
and becomes as it comes to be known:
in its moment of being known, it turns
to a painting where the world
is gathered in the form of a ship
coming into harbour far beneath us
from the mouth of sunset. The silent
poem: the moment of repose
before the mind, changing, throws the verses
down into strangeness. Then their silent god, once more
invisible, has to go back
to singing to be heard again.

30 April 2015

High Windows

This is the job
that finally
they gave me:
in spring, in autumn
to sweep up the bodies
of finches
around the bases
of the crystal-windowed
towers.

When I used to sleep
on the streets,
it was similar: one of us
died, the body
would be picked up
but as long as we lived,
never.

It was as though
there were someone somewhere
who said: Let them live.
Let them be
always. Let them
alone. Let us have them
with us
as they are
forever.

So strange it was,
and seemed, at first:
one of us disappeared,

no trace, or just
the filthy crumpled
bag of stuff
left in a corner,
but where was she?—until
it ceased to appear,
so often it happened,
a wonder.

Seasonal work,
a job for a while,
to search the long planters
and bases of the walls for birds
who break against windows
in the times of migration:
unable to see
the hardness in the shining
image of the new
more perfect world's
openness.

In the future there are people
who will have to imagine
what world these
words of mine
are living in—imagine it
from their day
in which there is no longer
the knowledge of what
were towers.

2 May 2015

The Glimpse

She lay down on the long cedar bench in the sun,
the wood glistening brown as if oiled. Careful for her face,
she folded her white silk scarf and laid it across
her forehead, eyes and nose, and felt the light
on her lips, felt the shape of her lips warmth-sculpted,
a living carving of a flower. The breeze fluttered
the down on her arms, she felt it, and it fluttered
the low whitish-green of the not-yet-blossomed sedum
around her, the carpet of the garden. I'll open and pull
my dress down to my hips, she thought. Just a few minutes
in the pool of the sun won't burn me, and neither will I
burn anyone, since I'm alone here.

There's no such woman.
I made her up, at first to avoid saying, "I—it was me"
when I sang about lying down in the sun. But it didn't work,
she became real, and as I lay there surprised and all at once
dreaming a poem where before there'd only been peace,
only warmth...as I lay there inventing her
to disguise me, I felt her breasts on my lean chest
pull outward and downward in the air and light
that touched them. I felt her knowledge of them, a sweet worry,
and then she decided to take off her dress completely
just for an instant. Then the air and sun, the coolness
and brightness of that day, washed into her and flowed
out of her freely as it does with a woman swimming.
The unfelt water that is always making her
palpably entered her, coming and going
like the ocean in the tide pools
or evening over the beach—the beach of the sky
with its long orange, carnation, and lavender dunes

over the beach of land and ocean
and small crabs skittering there in the almost dark:
the ideas of the moment.

                                        But maybe that's not the way
it really is, only the way a man imagines it
and wants it. Maybe in fact it's more rich or more plain and better.
My sister, so human you are, so much I love you with me
on our native land, that I can't wish you
freedom from death or knowledge. You'd fly, then,
far away from here, our home, far away from me,
and then what would we be? So I only wish you
that your body never hurts you. And the wish requires
that our world never hurts you: the world that makes up
your body—you are the birds and beasts and trees
and men. So you have to glimpse, when gripped
in the failure of age, or on any day like this one,
the dream of things at play in the fields of pleasure,
the way we did for a second as we lay on the cedar bench
in the sun. The scarcely remembered dream, the world as it is.
The glimpse must grow gaze in you.

9 May 2015

CHILDHOOD FRIENDS

Names of Birds

Awake at dawn, recalling my father, crying,
unable to go to sleep again, and soon
the first bird sings. Despair: when the first bird sings
and the first light comes and you haven't slept.
I curse myself: the many-noted melody
is its signature but I can't read its name.
My father knew the name of every bird,
every tree, bush, and grass they played in,
every seed, bug, and worm they ate. Their friend.
I've lived to an age far past what he received
and I know nothing. Father, where are you
so I can ask you and have you give me the names?
I always thought I'd take the time, later,
to learn them from you. A scientist, he used to say
names are only for people. Now I see
birds have names and he knew them. Not just
the nomenclature of kinds—the name of each one,
a strange sort of word that exists only an instant
when the bird answers a man who whistles to it
and then goes silent, hoping to hear him again.

11 May 2015

All One Limit

No word desolate enough
comes to me. No word that cries through the page
the way this light drizzle cries through the fledgling
green of May trees. The way the word of the sun,
diffused, impossible to find precisely, cries
through the glowing dun of an overcast
rounded from limit to limit. All one limit:
the sky screwed down on the earth like a bottle top
of chalky plastic. The grey underneath me,
divulged in the drains from its tomb of slush
by spring, and raised by desolation
to the sky, as the new sky. No word
desolate as your being elsewhere and the fear,
almost knowledge, that you could never
be happy with me could you
be here.

15 May 2015

Baltimore May 2015

Baltimore oriole singing from the tip
of a vast, spreading silver maple, and then
he goes quiet and flies, "swift as arrow," deep
into neighbour trees—his gold and blue
hardly visible up under the dazzling
dull sky. Last week they were burning Baltimore,
the never solaced wound of the African
never let heal, chains and bullets, the angry
contentment of the others schooling themselves hard
in the delusion: then is then and now is now.
The rose-coloured crab apples are almost done
with snowing: they're clouds mostly green,
though over there a hungry sparrow can knock
a flurry of pink out of one. But the white crab tree
still is fresh, dropping nothing, dense,
and opening inward—indescribable thought-like
ways of passage among petals
for the air it freshens. Behind it: the closed,
quiet house front: a face of supreme
beauty pondering, with a look, all outward,
that doesn't know or care how it looks. Under
the hedge, the gold forsythia flowers on the sidewalk
are skirts with empty central hollows awaiting
minuscule waists, a new human, girls
an inch tall, incorruptible, and somewhere already
dancing and laughing, naked, tasting each other's
lips, breasts, thighs, and the closed spaces
where frills and openings hide—the way
the wrinkled bark, the groins of limbs,
the passages to the interior of the tree,
all hide in the white petals. The way that the coming

race of humans, all female still in early embryo,
unthreatened, couples now,
beyond sight,
in a long-lost scripture, not yet written,
in the orgy of imagination.

18 May 2015

The Unemployable: An Essay on Isolation

Everything's happy
when it has to meet its purpose. Anxiety
harries humans, they say: evil need, purpose,
drives them in fear of poverty,
whereas the seed has no dread
as it advances upon its bursting and
vanishing into something else, and the fruit
doesn't worry about dying
and being eaten. But anxiety is a form
taken in man's heart by what in the seed
is need to meet its function. A ruined form:
need reft of desire. And yet, you need, you have
to get to the meeting in time through the gluey air
of your pain, your longing
to watch the morning light creep up
the flaking bark forever. You have to
go to the desk or the city won't be built
as badly as it is, your indescribable
and useless crumb of it. It will fall
further apart. You have to bring
the proceeds back to the hungry nest.
Only the one who can be compared
to a maple key
fallen in the asphalt gutter is free
from anxiety, not having
to be anywhere, and unhappy, for this one,
having no function, knows
he is certain not to breed
with the human soil, whose beautiful gaping
and strange odour of a shut-up freshness
longing to escape can be sensed

just over there, across the sidewalk. Only
the one who can be compared to this
key rain-pasted to the greyness,
as good as dead, never to unlock anything,
owns the wealth of stopping to look at it
as the body—corpse and corpus—of beauty.
Only this one, disconnected, looks with despair
on his riches. Everyone
is a word. Some fall on paved-over ground.

mid-May 2015

Philosopher and Southern Ohio

Praise those who finding themselves
alive on earth
pick up the work. Day after day
it never ends except that they call death
heavenly rest, and feel no guilt
in accepting it, as long as it comes late,
after a long or hard enough term of bearing
with the pain of the others. Only to die young
is a weakness, almost a sin—so fair
in a song it can make them cry. Praise them,
they hammer in a mine days and nights
and in the times remaining drive a mule
and an iron-prowed wood plough
on a steep slope for food. They help to poison
their own streams. They blame
themselves only, and jealously, joyfully
singing, they preserve the old way
of those who blame themselves. Their God
is innocence—he doesn't exist as I
would require him to and still he makes
the truth of the world be the dandelion
that the eyes fall on as a breeze starts
freshening summer, and the man towels his forehead...
the long road of dawn as he comes up
at shift's end...the people all together
for the dead friend at a hilltop churchyard
with shadows of the circling hawks
sweeping their feet...the ugly people
all saints, the community in one place
around the body...But no more rest.
The straggle of stores and cabins

under green ridges came, struggles
to maintain itself, later will be gone.
They never rest except for death
and they do not think the worry that spoils sleep
and the fear that twists dreams
are forecasts of the content of oblivion.

21 May 2015

To the Reader

This prayer I write as a poem because I know
very well I do not pray. A broken
willow reflects in the pool
the river partly turns aside to and enters
here just for a moment. One of its great stems
is fallen in the water, a sign of a century's damage,
which finally killed; a leaving, this May,
of a February storm. Or maybe just of a quiet
culmination, a crack, a slump with no one
to see or hear, after decades of seasons:
the arrived sum of the events of a long
flourishing and failing. It broke
and now it lies in my gaze with the rest
of the beauty there, in the quiet commotion
of memory and thought. Who can this anxiousness
be addressed to but you? A prayer
should signify a god, but even so little as you
may not be there: you'll have to read
this poem to exist. And what it signifies,
the agglomeration of a moment
belonging to someone else: can it be
anything for you? I beg you,
a person like me, baffled like me,
content in the intervals between the peaks
of terror, to go on my way, I beg you.

28 May 2015

Before Definition

First in the mind there should be
no words. Let poetry have a place
before definition, hammered signs,
inanities, greetings: those loves, those sweetnesses
congealed. A place without
coprophilia of a slang lost to honour
and humour. A space without the knowledge
that kills all the dandelions—they're weeds,
they're clones—in the flat buzzing corral
that makes the sun remorseless. Mind, place
of no words while the words are growing
invisible in the death and dream of sleep.
Mind, space for the turning
of a corner into the unexpected
world: the expanse before
it has said its prayer to you,
its commandment, its begging: Decide.

1 June 2015

The Twins

In the stories of America,
which almost no one in America knows,
the twins go down to the dead.
There, the world's a narrow cave,
a tunnel. There the air
is a dusty web. The kings sit along the walls
apparently for ages without moving or speaking
in two dusty rows facing each other.
They are like two ranges of barren unimpressive hills.
They are like two mummified lines of paratroopers
crouching in the hull of a plane that crashed
and lay for centuries at the bottom of an ocean
that dried up in the infinitely long
cataclysm of the earlier world, the one before
anything yet existed
in the human form that now exists. Here
is where those twins went willingly,
the heroes, daring death.

early June 2015

Love Poem

Did I ask you, did I assault you,
demand that you come with me, that you give,
you open up, you take, receive
from me what I want
to give you, that you lie
beside me always when I want?
You beat me. You stayed still and silent
longer than I flailed and cried. I continued,
moving away to where you were
nothing and built a world
out of the symbols of your smiles, the grey
green of your eyes, your fading
into evening, your words that ceased
to sound and became scripture,
tradition, a scrap of paper
tied with blue. Your smiles,
eloquent as the visage of a cat
and a star. I've been lying
morose a long time, a tangle
of grey worms, limbs on a bed
in the midnight of what's the use, what
was it all for, where it doesn't matter
that you won't answer, where asking
can only be for whatever you wanted
or the wind brings. Which is,
I guess, this emptiness
and a world that in some unimaginable
idea of yours
ought to be:
where anger is mildness,
the blank openness of all the possible,

the beneficence of making, letting
me go, go and find, such anger is love.

8 June 2015

Childhood Friend

I am condemned now
to my idea of you
but forever and forever
you call me out.
Albert! you call
at the time of dawn's
reaching up
into the treetops—come
out and play! And I leap
to your girl's voice,
the adults still sleeping.
And often too I'm the first
to get up and sneak away
and I'm the one who calls,
calls at your door,
a whispered shout, afraid
to wake your mother and father,
and you're asleep but soon
you come down.

                                        How my heart
sings even today
that it's you who've come down
for me. We'll go out
into the light that clothes itself
in dew sparkling across
lawns, trees, and flower beds:
our old world again. We'll run,
clothes all askew, as usual
with children no one has dressed,
and, running, we'll tear off

those shorts and shirts the moment
we get past the blackberry brambles
and into the woods, and laugh
over our different bodies
and inform each other all about them
solemnly. There's our hut of leaves
some bushes wove, there's the blackbird
and the garter snake,
goldfinch and grasshopper, and the huge
black and gold sun-in-shadow:
the garden spider; there's the carp
still in the reeds.

Yes you
called me out, you who've receded
into womanhood and godhood,
hidden behind the noon
and the starry night sky,
somewhere over the curvature of earth,
and my wondering, the doubt
if you ever were
or were a dream,
if any god
was in you, and if you grew
once I no longer saw you
into an anxious occupation
by the law that wills a death
for the trees and the birds
but two deaths for each of us,
woman and man. But you
called me out.

29 June 2015

Weed Trees

In the green everything is broken and confused
between the white ovoids of the tank farm
and the tracks, their silver stripes worn bright
and their grey slag.
                                        Dead branches twist
from every madly flourishing tree
in the thin line, and the wild grape
mounds and gaps on the fence of wire.
I could, I suppose,
write the algorithm of the rhythm
of the viper bugloss living low and blue,
scattered and huddled, around the ankles
of Queen Anne's lace and overtowering
some white daisies.
                                        Spindly azure, deep violet,
exploding spider stars, polypi, networks of fissures
to the fire cry of a twilight
glowing on this: world's pith or pit.
                                                                How children
love these waste lands I remember
now: wonderful earth of running and shouting,
the next best thing to space unguarded, these forgotten
in broad daylight or moist twilight miseries
with a creation in them—trees waving and
moss on broken
scattered junk, concrete blocks, ruins:
enough to give the children sight of the
ground of their play,
the open city, the green.

2 July 2015

The Corral

I think about something. Immediately
a corral is formed, where horses I own
are playing, or standing at ease, muzzles to the grass,
or nuzzling. A human can never tire
of looking at their eyes, the all-absorbing:
to see them and know and not know what they see
and to see them forevermore, every moment,
in your dream, working or sleeping: that eye
of the horse, rabbit, or trout: gentle and ready
for violence, accepting, a terror in suspense,
sorrowful, blank. All creation's eye of a girl
just coming to know the love of the world
that wants her is a brute thing. My horses
are playing with some others I've never seen:
the fence is broken somewhere. But the corral
is closed enough that there's a different Eden
within it than elsewhere. Daisies and clovers
that scarcely grow beyond its limit,
a different mix and density of golden flies,
more swallows that chase above them. My animals
have cropped and fertilized the ground
into many homes for all who could scarcely live
in the infinite home outside. The hawks
pass over the gates far above and the songs
of the crickets easily penetrate my corral.

20 July 2015

The Stag

As I stood looking at the head
of the great stag
my hounds had torn apart,
I saw that it was me
and I was dead.

They'd torn every part of it,
the fur was gluey, matted
and brown where it had bled.
The eye that looked at me,
mild and sorrowful, was my eye,
the forest's eye
in the bloodless head.

It had once been given me
to see everything
and to run through every entrail
of the naked wood.
My pack, that had terrified the wood,
where had it gone?
All was quiet. I was dead.

23 July 2015

My Garden Now Of

My garden now of nodding onion,
upland white aster, tick seed, and black-eyed Susan.

If I walk in my garden now with you,

you gone many thousand miles,

if we walk together here because the flame
that comes from earth into the soles of my feet
(my root or the image of my root), arising
into the spine, to the blossom
of open eyes and the cavern
space of mouth that is felt hollow,
cool and damp at the base of my tongue,
in the dark of the brain—

the flame in the root builds
the edifice of
this garden,
this walking,
this life together we don't have,

and we can walk there in the words of the true life…

while you're not here? What kind
of paradise is that? That
we go on
happy in the words
in the closed lost book
where I put them
if anyone will find them

and resurrect them with new delight
as we walk from those reading eyes
into the more dilated
and now more assured beating
of that heart?

Or no one
will ever find the words again
but we and our moving
happiness will be there
in the dark of the book—what kind
of paradise is that? What inhabits
the song of desire composed
as longing's completion,
especially lost, whether despised or more simply
never noticed? What we want
is our body, the beautiful: to sing
that song and perpetual
wondering with our mouths. Not
to live in a song but live and sing among
nodding onion, upland
white aster, tick seed,
and black-eyed Susan. O words
of hope and perfecting, forgotten
as soon as made,
reveal your meaning.

10–19 August 2015; 30 March 2016

To Cross Over into Camp Fire

Once the fire has leapt upon its fuel
and we are sitting round it
with our marshmallows
skewered on sharpened sticks
and out beyond the veil of the border of glimmer and darkness
among the marsh mallows at the swamp's edge
some frogs boom a humble love
made solemnly and briefly in cold and darkness,
the fire will not die. One half of it
departs for the sky through its sharp
wavering point the way a word
part understood, part mistaken, part
deeply welcomed, part a troubling
desperately refused,
changes slowly in the digesting heart
of the hearer. The other half
moves horizontally into our happy chatter.
Let it not be selfish! Let talk not forget
all who have no fire tonight,
as one day we will have no fire,
we'll lie in the dullness, the last
ember—in the third half of fire, the ash, with little left
but the fire that fled above, the measure that went up
from the flame tips to live in darkness
as cold points defining
a wish that the happy elsewhere
should not forget us.

appx. 10 August 2015

Sudden Little Parade Downtown

The first tall flower-encrusted wagon appears
in the fastfood restaurant window and the eaters
lower their burgers. Look! The street

is filled with honey-gold people suddenly
and the motors are gone, the panel trucks, SUVs,
high-end sports cars with their subtle low riffs

of burps. Now the sound is chanting, tinkling,
bells and rattles. South Indians fill Yonge
and some whites go along the fringe, the curbs,

with camera goiters at their necks. *Hare Krishna,*
Hare Krishna, Krishna Krishna, Hare Hare,
Hare Rama, Hare Rama, Rama Rama, Hare Hare

floats in the air softly as voice and drumbeat,
and ripples embroidered in brilliant Roman letters
on a breeze-lifted banner hung on the back of the float.

Behind it, a long interval of strolling chatting
celebrants—call them worshippers? devotees?
believers?—and then here comes a second wagon,

another long stretch of people, then a third...
Each a whole story tall and all in flowers,
a curved canopy atop and girls in robes

peeking out of its mouth, and in front of them
a chubby sage in Buddha lotus pose,
enveloped in saffron and fanned by a big man

with an enormous placid feather. The sages wave
impassibly to the watchers. O Hinduism, mosaic
of gods and stories, intricated bits

of colours—stars!—baffling, pleasing, many
as the flowers cladding the wagons. Your world is
the tesserae in the basin of a great fountain,

with its scenes of creation, war, destruction, triumph,
in the palace courtyard, all things a patchwork
of celebration sketching heedless joy

of the dark and light god. The patches having been cut
from the people's misery and doings. A beadwork,
innumerable beads, like a wampum of treaty

with the power that reigns over poverty,
treaty that every day saves and gives us back
the body, which reigns over pleasure.

niyawee honiyawe hane
niyawee honiyawe hane'eh

Singing the dream song of the maker
who dwells in the sky, singing every day
the miraculous escape, the rescue.

Ka mate, ka mate! ka ora! ka ora!
Ka mate! ka mate! ka ora! ka ora!
Tēnei te tangata pūhuruhuru
Nāna nei i tiki mai whakawhiti te rā
Ā, upane! ka upane!
Ā, upane! ka upane, whiti te ra!

A step upward from the trap, the pit, another
step upward, the sun shines! Hinduism,
will you live? The street you come along says no.

You won't find any elephants there but the small ones
painted in blue on the white rims of the ten-foot-high
gently ongoing wheels of your three wagons. How

will you speak with only memory,
no elephants, to be your words? The street fills
back up with shoppers, now you're gone,

and the cars return as the parade
moves out of earshot south
toward Lake Ontario.

21 August 2015

The Mural

Here's my name. The stand of purple thistles
partly hides some of us, growing
from the crack between the sidewalk and the cement wall,
right at the spot down low where we signed ourselves,
Mural Crew, then our names in a sloppy stack.
Here I am: Mischa Benevides-Chan
just above Debbie and below Giancarlo—
where are those two? Where are they all?

Ten of us that summer—the City got us from school
to decorate the north side of the underpass:
"to beautify the neighbourhood and express
the local culture," something like that, a City
"initiative" back then, dropped with the next election,
when the government changed. We were all in art class
in the high schools around there. We knew each other
a little, in twos and threes. It was a stupid project
but we flew with it. We caught on fire
there in the shaking and noise of the trains
going over our heads every five minutes—
I never had such friends as that summer.

Doesn't look to me now like we had much talent:
it's crummy children's art, like a five-year-old
drawing a house, a tree, a flower, and the sun
in crayons. And yet, it's not. How they grew, I remember,
out of our laughing and talking, out of our fingers—
this line of boxes, some with peaked roofs,
to stand for the long rows of stores and houses,
with the business names badly printed in black
on the untrue brightness of the facades, the atom-bomb

blaze in the colours. Turn around, look up down
the street and the cross streets—most of the models
are still here: the liquor store, the Yummy Bar-B-Cue,
the Turkish pizza place, Jenny's Tavern with the old
scrawny white guy smoking outside, the rec centre
with its little garden of flowers and benches. I think
the same posters, a bit more sun-faded now,
are still pasted in the window of the beauty parlour,
the same sign for braided extensions, the same list
of the same cheap prices. How our stick figures,
red, blue, green, purple, jump
and dance along the roofs,
arms spread—stars, starfish—they seem to be running
like lovers seeing their lovers suddenly,
running into the arms of our huge floating flowers
that look to me like leaves, mouths kissing
or calling, like comets. The gold-hot day
of our sun, up in the corner, doesn't veil them
but brings them out to swim with it through the blue,
with the check marks of birds and the black crosses
of the telephone poles, to help it with the day.

We'd kneel painting and hear the streetcars whoosh
just behind our backs, and ideas, satisfaction,
questions, and more ideas spilled
back and forth as we looked straight ahead and drew
on the white cement with its one figure,
"1953," engraved high up above us
in an oblong box. Every one of them
left this neighbourhood and went beyond
my knowing. Like my husband did later. Probably
like my sullen druggie kid will soon. I was thinking
of sneaking back here at night sometime
with a bottle of black and a thin brush and work gloves

for pushing the sharp thistles back, and repainting
the fading names. But then I thought: there's never
nobody out on this street, and a chittering line
of toddlers went by me, roped together, with their teenage
counsellors in lavender t-shirts
wrangling them to the lakefront or some park,
and I said to myself: let it be as it is.

late August 2015

OUR OWN DARK HANDS, IN THE RECESS OF OUR LOVE

To the Soul

I made the mistake of wanting
the woman that I love
to be as you are always
naked, amorous, young,
and though shy to others, to me
always opening, always
desiring, demanding me.

Sometimes the woman's tired
or satisfied, as I am—she wants me
to lead her naked on a golden chain
through the busiest streets
sometimes: but only sometimes.
The woman lets me rest,
you never. To save myself I try
withdrawing, but I have to see you,
abandoned Ariadne, self-stripped always
and crying on the beach. How beautiful
your breasts and eyes to the man
who would see you from the sea,
your naked back and open hips
to the man who approaches by
the grassy dunes. How weak,
how sporadic my powers to your
endless hunger, your pain. The first
words at the closing of the door
of paradise, when delight survived
but the omnipotence of the body
had been taken away, I know: Thank
God for the woman.

31 August 2015

Man Changing into Thunderbird

(Norval Morrisseau; 1977; five large panels; Art Gallery of Ontario)

I want to be the sort of thing I am, a man,
but it's not possible anymore.
Nevermore. Does the thunderbird have to say it
like the English raven? I see my eye
wide open, circular, staring, a bird's eye,
a fish's eye. To fly in the water,
peer from the air, the rock ledges, the open grass
or coverts of bush. To watch,
wary, ready, and see no one knows what:
I no longer know what, though I can see
the five changes in the
waterfall of the change.

How I became the bird, and the conduits,
the threads, the knowledge, the veins
that stretched between us
when I still was: when the bird and I
were still two, within one body: were organs
of the air. I can still see now
how it was then, and how it would become
only the bird, the bird they say was never.

Only the bird and still a man, knowing
as only the bird knows, with no
idea. Or no other idea. It would not be
different from this knowledge of dawn,
cold dawn, waking up on the gravel,
the no-knowledge of the spindly
blue flower
right in my eye, right by my drooling mouth

burning motionless
while on the tracks these
thoughts grind and rattle by.

                                                    It would not be
different from me except as every
thoughtless
thing is only that moment bird
and flower. I'll get up
and paint this. In this
loneliness here I am half
dead.

Summer 2015

Dream

Dream
dream of day
girls and boys
ungoverned

in their peace
of the coasts where the contention
is of spume
crests of breakers
spindrift
with the blood-and-
honey-streaked
white
eucalyptus flowers

or their peace
of inland valleys
where the foam is
the hulls of clouds
brushing the oak crowns
above the blossoming
almonds and apples

Dream
dream of night
where your father
a naked female clown
bent with age
the lips of the vulva

sunk
in greying beard
your father
the naked female clown
with bloody mouth
stands waiting
halfway up
the infinite marble
stairway to the base of the
nonexistent
monolith
and your girl
lost to you
how long how long
you see her
across the scrawl
of wedding guests
with white curtains
blowing dancing
happy ghosts
at the French doors
open on the forested slope to the river
and the two of you
see
back from death
in the same instant
leap up
begin to make your way
to each other
through the crowd

Dream
dream of day
dream of night

to be released
                    from the old
man the first
                    man brooding
his crimes and losses never
to be forgiven
                    dream in the key
of mercy the key
of colour and light
dreaming
              to be released
from carefulness
into the new
human

3 August 2015

Escape to the Sea

1. Escape to the Sea

The ancient heroes longed only to stay home.
Or to reach home
across the sea. Did they fail to see,
raised on the edge of the sea,
wielding the sword edge, burning towers, by the sea,
burying comrades on the sea beaches, the blood
in the rivers flowing down to the sea,
weeping, roasting meat around fires next to the sea?

The sea was their only home.
The sea is no home to a man.
Much wandering sours and estranges his heart,
the sea is the desert, the living sea,
dead to a man, it will kill him, with its fishes,
its many fabulous citizens, its cold,
its black twistings like his dreams,
the vast expanses, little different ever,
slowly shifting, the bitter storms, come and gone,
impossible to remember except as dread. The vast
expanses and wandering them in the coffin hull,
and soon not even his body is a home,
it drifts or he rows it threatened or lets the sails
drag it flying over the treacherous
vastness that he is.

If only I could live in a tiny house
of sod and stone, a brief distance inland,
and there my voice inside me could talk with her
and with the land, so that when I grew stiff

with dwelling and I walked and mounted the dunes,
the sea
would dawn as a great freedom, the clean billowing
of the bedsheet, of the sail.

2. The Road: Homage: Cormac McCarthy

The great gate of the shore,
the black gate, the gate where, beyond,
the sun was always burning
mildly in its frame, the sun
low to the earth, a dawn or dusk,

the gate where the one who stood looking
in its terrible arch, trembling to move beyond,
to cross through it, always saw inward
the promised city
from his wilderness, and always saw outward
from the jumbled city he longed to leave
the green world, the distant
sparkling stream there beyond...

the prophet closed the gate
and then annihilated it. The shore
in his words ceased to be
a fringe of freedom
where we could stand
before freshness. Before mere power
clothed in the simplest diaphanous shift,
the first element, veiling
what? what body?

The jumble of the city now
lay spilled on the shore,

its disease filled the immobile waves.
There on the sand we found
lay a man just recently become a corpse
who had struggled across the vacant lot.
His son is crying
in the immense vista
with no one. Eternity
has changed: no more
the marriage of the one who died
to the sea that lives within the sea
and before it, but the terror and pain, everlasting,
of the one left alone.
To have to live.

10 October 2015; May 2016

The Commandment of Love

In the law and logic of desire "I
want" is converted into what should be
and everlasting into everlasting.

The furious springs of motion everywhere
lie still within the measure of their fury
as what should be appears as what has been.

"I want" is seen for the other name of law
and heard as final speaking of the law,
which is completed in its name. The earth,

the inner and the outer fires, the core,
the stars, mute lives and spaces have no law,
being what they do and suffer. This takes form

as law in me and you. What murder buds
identical with innocence in us!
So you and I lie far apart forever

knowing that only man and woman can teach
the gods more than the chaos of the law.
And so the long groping crafting of our love.

21–23 November 2015

Our Dark Hands

There is no way, dear one, to avoid
the circle of our luck.
In the blue globe of your flocks
of birds flying over
in the last gold stretched between your green crowns
we're still and we talk,
even if dying, consumed in peace.

*

What does it mean to talk to you
who have no voice? I love you,
the distance-sweetened caws and screeches,
the soft twitterings of vast flocks
invisible in your oaks, the nearly inaudible swell
of your bodiless sea in the leaves. I derive
nothing from this. I love to hear you,
to listen hour after hour, to return
day after day to our bench
and listen again. What I have is words. You derive
nothing from them and come
every day, every year,
and listen again. We're together,
we are one moving to become one,
the illusion of understanding
on the way to understanding.

*

Your voice will never die.
That is to say I'll hear it

even in the silences that are
to rest, consider, recollect,
and then, picking up once more,
our talk will never die.

*

Poetry is made in a bed like love:
made as love is made, in a bed
that is love. And while it's made,
all vision of the misery of the world
is shut out. Here as we talk
the misery of the world is far away
in us, and quiet in us. Is it here?
Is it like light in the darkness
when your sun goes out
and my mind strays? The screams somewhere,
the blank dwelling in the squalor far away:
are they the dark in the sun here
when the leaves we love
shelter us, and their strange rustling
in the midday twilight,
their wall outside of which the noon
stalks us, at bay—when the dark hands that love
and save us bring no pleasure,
bring us fear? Our own
dark hands, in the recess of our talk.

11 October 2015

ART OF SURGERY

The Fount of Every Name

If I recall you and call you
Eurydice, if I keep your name silent
and call you by hers, the ancient bride of song,
the first lost belovèd in the brief
millennia of our memory, endless road of losses…

even if I take Eurydice and make her
new, with a new voice
and a different nudity, yours,
so far as my mind can approach your voice and nakedness
now that my hands
can't move across your body
ever again…

Forgive me that I give you a name,
Eurydice. Only a word for a history
men and women know, if badly,
can be a word and say you
in some way we understand, the way the light
needs a thing to fall on to be light.

Even though you are the fount of every name,
your name we won't know. We scarcely know
the beauty of our names
pointing to yours where it sits among them silent
as though lost. With you it went down to the past
and now with you it lies
no longer behind but underneath
to be searched for in the earth.

11 October 2015

The History of Grief

When I decline it will be
terror and long pain for you,
long even if it's short, and helplessness
and confusion. You won't know what to long for
till I die, and then finally you can rest, you'll think,
and you'll curse yourself for that thinking.
Every colour, remaining itself, will be grey,
the people, trees, and buildings, near
as ever, will be infinitely distant,
a city in a cold lake, drowned,
in a dream. You won't know where to be
or how to place your limbs. Slowly, then,
the action of your body
will carry you back to life. The horror
will turn sporadic: pools on the beach
in the tidal ebb of a poisoned ocean.
At last you'll remember me happily.
The pain will have withdrawn
and will sound far off. And then
when you decline, I won't be here
to have that same long pain and confusion
for you and after you die to spin and wander
like something that no longer belongs
to this world. I won't be here for the wildness
in me to subside slowly to peace
and gratitude. You won't have this one,
your other one, as I did, here in this world
to remember you happily.

21–22 October 2015

The Wanderer

Dweller in the house
yearning after me as I go by,
yearning to be on the road, like me,
free and alone, I know well that you are more
an exile, a wanderer, than I am,
and on my two feet, weariness
and not knowing, I am the one more at home.

23 October 2015

Reverie

As I slowly approach the opening
of the long entrance to sleep,
death waits at the far end to take
the memories I am as they turn
into fantasies and blending shapes.
My loves and dreams that I hope some day
to finish and exalt: sleep finishes them
each night, cutting them off in the midst
of their failure and laying them back
in not-being-anymore. They start again
tomorrow and reach the same
inconclusion, eddying out into drafts
of colour, voices, melting times and bodies,
then the blank. Sleep completes
my futile revisions so I can take up my loves
freshly at dawn. Dying: last of these drifts
into dark, last cut-off of these gestures
toward making perfect, or enough, or something,
of what I lived.

                                  Or death is sleep
of a still greater tenderness than this. A huge house
in which, as in the tiny mortal house,
the souvenirs are handled lingeringly,
then put aside with the plan to bring them out
some day when there will be time
to treasure them truly. A day that never comes. And then
the inheritors or buyers throw them away…
or even the first owners, since now
in the mortal house there's no room left to keep them.
But in death there's plenty of room.

Everything's kept. Even the rememberer forgets—
the small circle of his regard shines
only here and there on his field of things.
But death always visits them and loves them
all at once. It waits ages, universes, for him
to fall asleep remembering his little
so that he can wake up later in the long ungrasped
holding of her hand.

3 November 2015

Love, Thou Art Absolute Sole Lord

The poet says that love informs
and governs every body, act
and motion. And he's right.
"All things seek all things
without rest." A flower seeks the black
whirlpool with the still pit
of loss at centre. The law
of dissolution seeks the thing
to marry it, as Iseult sought Tristan.
There is this power, the deepest skeleton
wrought into the centre
and shape of flesh and bone:
it encloses and holds up
space and time as a scaffold does,
as a mother's look. But, love, this love
comes from me alone.
I am its only house. And only you
can say the same. Love, you and I
thought up and built what came
before us and is in everything,
everything. I loved you. So the war
that tore us into scraps, and razed down
our family, all sign and memory of us,
was nothing. And there is no nothing,
only this world ever more world
because I love you.

5 November 2015

Art of Surgery

The hands that know the mechanism
the way a pianist knows or an engineer,
and the mechanism that they know,
a slimy leaping heart
struggling, with its loves and fears this hour
in the abeyance of drugged sleep—the hands that know
the heart can't stop to be worked on or it disappears…it becomes
too visible, a still lump
inside a fallen formation
without the dignity of stone.

The pianist has to bring skill
back from the desert of ability
to the ghost in the manuscript
crying with thirst
to be a city again. The engineer
has to bring mathematics back to a home,
the philosopher leads the scattering words,
the poet reins a bucking image to charge
in violent loveliness at fact. Let all workers
arrive exhilarated from their tasks. The surgeon's love
hands back the readjusted mechanism
to the lover of my body. Let me bring her once more
my own hands' power to stir.

6 November 2015

Descent to the Dead

In so far as I transform myself
into my song, I can live again
forever, although the song
will be dead as this body's dead,
lying by itself in the dark, the shut
book, drying out. Yet the song can be resurrected
at any time by anyone—by you—
the body, not. The song needs only someone,
not God. And God doesn't need to resurrect
the song because he hears it
always, as we say: just as he doesn't need
to resurrect our bodies. He knows
and loves them unchangingly; it seems
he raises them for us, who can't.
Left to ourselves we would lie in filthy
silence and self-contempt. He appears
in you in the form of your will
to hear the dead song: your will mostly defeated
in wandering the buzzing maze
of every day. The song
needs only paltry you to live. It wants
to catch the blood of your wandering
attention, drink it, give it
a body. It wants
just a moment, a moment of a repeated
descent to the dead
that your life can make, your life,
which in so far as it descends
and listens
lives.

10–11 November 2015

Dream

Desolation: I'd passed
a long beautiful day with her—
was she my earliest love, was she death?
And then I realized:
we had run off together into a new life
and now it was the evening of the first day
when you, far from me, were seeing
that you'd been left alone. I couldn't
cry out to you. The universe grew black.
All meaning black.
Not nothingness,
just nothing but the feeling of a sorrow
never to be lessened, a harm
never to be undone.
Helpless love. You, the best
beloved and the most loving,
through me
the most alone.

25 September 2015

The Pond in the Woods

The man who was content with a still pond
and the reflection of the woods along its shore
became the rock beside its water—a rock
like a statue of a man reclining,
with something like a head here, something like a face,
the kind of face a flower is, or the front
of a woman's body. If you come here,
you'll continuously be provoked and soothed.
The world will be this crystal ball of space
and a dream. Maybe you'll "spill your seed,"
the whole silken place and silence entrancing you
like the entrance to a womb, and then,
excitement faded, you'll become as little moved
by all such linkings of living things as the man of stone
with the gaze of water. Then there will be no response
to you here anymore, except for this unmoving.
And later the itch for converse that drives you out.

7 November 2015

Vergil, Legend

Vergil, Legend: is there a shade
of difference between your two names
here in this twilight world where we wait
long ages, beside the empty road,
then see you travelling through?
We see you again, conducting still another
of the ones summoned by love
along the path we've walked a part of
with you, last summer—the part we have,
here, of the path you walk forever
and all of, since it is you. You always move
and stand at its every point, in sight,
our sight, and beyond. Among and through us
and past us, you lead the summoned.
We can't see clearly in the dusk: "Is this one
me," one of us says, "am I finally
travelling with him now, going farther
though I'm still here?" You, long familiar
with the whole way, assuage your companion's
astonishment as he looks at us
and hears these things. His fear and wonder
renews your own—you've heard us
so long and often. But the savour
of the secrets of hell and heaven
and the earth are only yours—are known
only to the one who walks it all, returning
again and again to guide the chosen, the needy,
and later to come back alone.

2 December 2015

Nazareth

Nobody much knows we're here,
my grandmother and me. Oh, my mother and father,
who parked me with her for today,
know it, and my sister and my brother,
who went off with them. The town knows my family:
builders and pavers with brick. So it knows vaguely
that we're here, I'm here.

Some of the old people
knew my grandfather, who founded the company,
welcomed newcomers from Italy, saw to it that quickly
they were citizens and voted, helped found a parish,
a friendly-and-insurance society, was a bank director
and a farmer. And I know about him: here's his marranzano
though his ocarina's lost now, with the songs he'd sing
on the stoop at evening; here's the strawberry barrel
that's from his time, and the great garage
that was a barn of his, not long before my birth:
a corner of it was for his shoemaker's bench,
his awls and disc-nosed hammers. The neighbourhood knows
we live here, and a few people all over town,
but outside the town no one at all.

Here I am
by the sunny western stoop, by the peach tree,
listening to the sparrows' excited debate
under the vine leaves. In the vine-framed window,
west side of the kitchen, Gram's making pizza dough.
We're apart, we touch, each closed in a separate sphere,
transparent, with a shell that can't be felt
yet can't be walked through. Whenever she hugs me

the two coincide almost entirely: my circle
of seven years, hers of a powerful
youth in old age with its treasures of far-come-from
times and worlds that arrive in lightning sparkles
from a half-opened chest.

But now, not touching,
far separate if close, both of us know—
me seeing her through the screen,
she at the counter, absorbed in her work—
that something great has happened with us,
just this moment: a shattering
we've felt together though apart, a vast and calm
eruption beneath our feet and skin, beneath
the bottoms of the wells of our hearts,
under the earth, sky, and inmost
centre of everything. Out in the world
no one knows. No one knows that we're here.

7 December 2015

The Year

The year: it runs from May to May
and all of childhood is preparation
and all of life an aftermath
for the year. In the first May, she comes.
And though you've known her all your life,
your eyes open. Your senses open
and you know her. In the second May,
she leaves. And now, the calendar is defined
for all humankind, for all of time.

Many years later she writes to you
from a billion miles away, seated
at the desk of her husband, her pilot
through empty space. "What children we were,"
she writes you, "when we thought our year was the measure
of everything, or of anything, even ourselves. I'm here
at the edge of two star systems in collision,
thousands of worlds destroyed: we would have said
'thrown into hell' in the self-centredness
of those old days. I know you regret
your failure with me. I'm sorry you were hurt.
Be at peace now. Everything was for
the best, or will be soon."

You recall that in the June
after the second May, when flowers,
gold and blue, were grey, you wrote a song
where she was a silver ship
in empty space, where infinite speed
is the same as paralysis. Only two human traces
remained to her there: a peach tree

planted on the surface of her hull, dead
after brief long suffering,
half burnt by a near star, half frozen
by the dark on the opposite side;
and in her cabin, diminished to nothing,
the clock of our world, its childish idiocy.

26–27 December 2015

THE ONE WHO ANSWERS THE CALL

The One Who Answers the Call

The little girl who burned in the burning house—
after the earthquake they carried her
from where they'd unburied her and across
the long field of blocks of rubble.

They had to get her to where a car could still reach,
to load her, and hurry her to the broken hospital
while they told her along the way to stay alive,
working on her, and she was dead, thank God.

Because of our science, we no longer can tell
just when she died. The doctors struggled to do
what they would never call "restore to life"
and then pronounced her dead. But we know

she died as they carried her to the car. She died
in the arms of the great man—thick mail of canvas
and asbestos—another mother, stumbling over fragments,
keeping his tears from falling on the little ash.

31 December 2015

Never to Be Exhausted

Never-to-be-exhausted
fascination of sunset.
Clouds that never move
and then have passed
far eastward, from rose to grey,
low to high. Slow melding
and decline of colours: you
hold a calm here whose blood is
perpetually still. You
slipping away of things invisibly
into another, another, never to be
exhausted, you die to rescue me
from the unending. In your mercy you turn
into black, and wondering
what world of colours-more-than-colour
within deep veins like planetary streams
among long buried mountain ranges
in a world without light Merlin
saw for a thousand years
inside the oak, I have to leave. The black
is merely black to me, except in dreams,
and only motion keeps me warm
in the dreariness, and you a friend
to meet again tomorrow.

15 January 2016

Gift, Distance

I watched myself go foraging. I saw me
cross the field, hesitating, glancing,
listening here and there. And then I
vanished in the covert
and re-emerged
with the bird of azure
in my teeth. Later I purred in the sun
and that night slept with my sisters
in our cave between the roots
watchfully, curled into the others
in the dark that's not obscure to me.

Then I drew back from myself again,
image, reflection, and body
giving each other the space we need
and in the blackness across this gift,
distance, two of us
discussed the day's happenings
and enjoyed the fire and stars
until we too fell asleep.

18 January 2016

Fair and Dark

The shower washed all the gold
out of your hair. You leant over the sink,
your buttocks with your bending
open, and removed your lenses: your eyes
burst from blue, went back
to their black again, fused into mine
in the mirror. Full, strong, soft, your body
took on once more the robe of your dusk—
purity of gentle contour: antidote
of the blonde, the meagre with its shoulder bones
sticking almost through, hip bones and pubic bone
threatening a thin and tight-pulled wrapping,
gold foil and filigree: the quasi-angel's
peekaboo of skeleton. You turned. Your breasts
heavy in the hands of light, your torso shining,
shaped with light—weren't they light? The source
of blood and birth was a child's mouth
lightly closed. The roughness
of the surfaces, the intricate braid
and beadwork of flesh in the damp
ruffling of lips within lips,
and the throat somewhere deeper...
the real angel
with its hoarse voice
announcing the terror of change
could just be heard there. As if the work
of eating, excreting, speaking, had been done,
had dropped away, not needed
now that the pure body
had been shaped by their purposes. Now
no child would again be born

because we were the child to come
from the lovers we were...or the phallus
was the child, full of anxiousness
to be grown, eager to know
everything that a man and a woman do, and so
stretching up between us, longing
to touch and smell and see...
And there would always be many children.

6 February 2016

The Universe

I know well that in some corner
of the universe as I hold
entirely within me
the whole universe, content in peace—
its story, its every gesture, every fragrance, every fact,
its explosion, its winding down—
there is a tiny part, a torn-off rag—me—
that is only suffering, only pain,
and doesn't know, can't know
that it is all of me and holds
the whole universe within it
in peace. And this piece
holds and hates the universe...
or simply is its central point unknowing,
its total contraction, animal sorrow.

14 March 2016

Pronunciation

Then poetry discovered the zero,
nothing: it is pronounced. Pronunciation,
which is to say the appearing of the god,
the appearing of what comes from nothing
out of the common air and sights of the world,
or out of blackness or blankness. Theophany
of a sound from silence. Poetry
was unsurprised to find this, except as it is always
surprised by everything. As always it began
to draw the corollaries of its finding. That zero
is pronounced requires—rechoirs,
said this science with a grin—that women and men
were there before zero to speak it, and all the long tradition
of verses running through famine and love
with the river sparkling under the window of the lovers
joined now at this moment and shrieking
for one last time—the dawn
has to divide them like a death and now the light
begins to seep toward their bed
through the eastern woods. The art of verse,
the woods and river, the whole earth,
its common sights that the lovers needed
so the world and word can be—all for the zero
to be pronounced. All, for the necessary !
to be added, giving breath the explosion, power
in one mind and body: to give the fact
of the 0 being voiced, O! in the body
of its sound. The sound of love in its making,
sound of the sudden
seeing of a hummingbird come
to a flower, or an eagle out of nowhere come

to a rabbit. When I lay beside you,
on you, under you, we were almost one. When the one
entered the zero, we were almost all,
the world was—O! look!—the total poem
all ready and being produced just now
for the first time
through the lips that are their cry.

29 March 2016

To Merwin

In the stirring of spring
I wanted my thought to be
as sweet as the wind.

*

The arguments inside me
took me away
from the sun-dazzle on the plain of snow.

The sparkling water
being set free from one form for another
and laughing in the gutters

receded to a backdrop
for my desperate staving off of successful
enemies at every gate.

*

In the great poet
it does not matter
that thought can't establish
the superior eternity
of the dream within the sun
dissolving the pure snow
in the sweetness of the breeze.
In our argument
our arguing, condemned to death, is equal:
the equal eternity of hell. In the great
poet the great is great and the arguments

are condemned to death. The dream
emerges from the vanishing of both:
the vanishing of the snow
permanent in his gratitude,
the argument melting at last
dying in giving birth
to nobility buried in it.

*

In the great poet
the beautiful instant
was perennial in me
as I walked along
distracted and dying, not noticing
my own mind
in my unworthy concern

which in the great poet is
my human need.

7 March; 16 April 2016

In the Past

No longer with me but I couldn't find you
in the past. In my myth of you,
you had looked behind, so in my thought
there we were: crying Orpheus kissing
the salt statue of Lot's wife. A state,
an image, but you were gone.

Behind was nothing. Now but far away
was nothing: another form of before.
I looked there. But you fooled me:
you came here. Suddenly. In dream,
in longing. You came here and now
were walking in my heart. You showed yourself:
you'd always been walking in my heart.
Your terror that I remember—"O God,
don't let me be old"—lives and all these years
had lived in me unseen,
calmly going on in you to its disaster.
I had loved and hated your fear. It was my life.

Fear of life is passion. You cross
the bridge of *is* from dread to suffering,
and the terror of pain is life. Is god,
as far as you know. It is a smooth expanse
in all directions. It stretches
its featurelessness out so gently
toward whatever else may somewhere be…
maybe it's flowing into us from there:
river so placid that it runs both ways
and remains. Water-heart of our land that seems
not even to beat anymore, as if the well-watered valley

could stay unmoved. A still rhythm,
a silent ripple reflecting the poor mills,
bridges, and houses in a light
that we, though you are not with me,
listen to tonight.

29 February; 16–17 April 2016

Then Demeter Gave

Then Demeter gave Persephone
the single seed, the tiniest one of all,
the infinitesimal. By it she'd always live
and return and be found, and there never
would come a time when you could leave her
a note in the house and not find later
her own note written under it:
never a time when you could not find it
because she was gone forever from the house
and present in it
only as truth, the eternity of memory.
Because of the seed there would always be
her pencil, her moving hand, and her grin,
as she saw what you'd written her
and answered it, and as she imagined you
coming back home once she'd gone
and reading the joke she'd made,
and as she thought how, finding her still away,
you'd do the same again
and so it would go, response
to response till the moment she and you
could be home at once. So Demeter gave
Persephone the smallest seed,
the indivisible,
the one as large as everything—as all
of time—which also can't be divided: but there is only
one thing that can't be divided,
the immense. So death too
may love Persephone
and she may go to him sometimes, they may

marry her to him, but she'll always be
with you.

14 April 2016

The Spot

From my homelessness I see my land
as a man in a place sees it, small and vast,
from his one spot. It may be where he's stopped
to pant in the infinite dryness of the sun
on the hard road, or the spot on the road where he happens
to be now as he walks
passing through. From it, he sees the people all
around him who live in the place,
and he sees the people who once lived here
in the birds, animals, flowers, crops, and mountains,
and he carries them: the stories of the place
in its moment now: streams flowing into a lake,
roads coming into a town. The place is his home.
What he thinks about it is his poem,
his world of grief tinged with happiness
or happiness full of mourning, that he makes
as he moves forward
and looks out at it, far around him,
from his homelessness, his spot.

17 May 2016

An Image of Our Life

Here's a house that was deserted—fled from
quickly or slowly in face of the war's advance,
and a shell split it after it was abandoned
(there are no cadavers) or the roof simply fell.

Here it is lying open, a smashed gourd
spilling its seeds. Or more like an open drawer,
too far opened, too quickly, hanging ajar,
rifled by scavengers, its contents thrown and scattered.

When you are relentlessly living, storing up
your precious objects—letters and photographs—
to be happy with what you lived and those you lost,
imagine this house. Here's a history, like yours

available to be cherished. Who will spend
his time to read it, to praise its loves. Will you?
It does not even exist, as far as you know.
You have to imagine it as never seen again.

*

This image of the house—
that everything disappears
into unknownness, the eternity
of memory most of all—

that disappearance
is indifference, inexhaustible
ocean that washes
the world clean

of things as a bone,
and is divine,
and to be saved or happy
you have to be content
the world will be cleansed
of you—

this devastating
image of the house
is the silhouette against the twilight
of a shepherd boy,

naked, though we can't make him out,
only an outline
up on a ridge
in a world now without shepherds.

The shepherd boy and his sweet
saeta of bitter sorrow
played on his flute and voice
in this twilight of dawn or nightfall,

we cannot know. His girl is gone.
Did she die, did they send her away,
did she prefer another? The song
doesn't say, and we listen
and we hear time,
time that is movement that draws apart,
time that is life, the only life,
time that is death.

Time. Beauty drawing away
and now gone. What lust we feel! What
would we do with him

if we could reach him? Lust,
lust, lust to put one arm
around his narrow shoulders,
to pat his curly hair—fellowship
with a child—to bend down
and kiss his crown once
as all he ever wanted eddies
in the song. The song that is content
in the placid coolness,
with the sheep lying
or grazing idly, the shuddering
quick rhythm of their breathing,
in a wide country, low hills
and cork woods and olive groves,
sparse grass, a world that is
his care, the only care
he gives, or ever could give.

Lust to touch him, but he is
an imaginary man. He is me.
If only I
could put my arms
around my shoulders
and bend down and kiss
my thick hair once
eternally.

*

You will not die. I'll never lose you.
So sang the shepherd boy,
too young almost to have memories,
to her, and in her to all
his memories, slow scattering sheep

grazing in the twilight,
some out of view, some
maybe lost, who knows yet?

So he sang in the shadow
of a broken hut,
and to the shepherds became a legend,
where someone had once lived,
where a love was lost
and the house decayed
and the story was forgotten, except
that a love had been lost.

I've often repeated it:
you will not die. And though in song
there are no therefores, in this song,
since you will not die,
therefore the earth will not die,
and your world will not die:
the buildings of the town,
decayed now, many vanished,
where you grew,
and the songs of those days, all
but forgotten, and the old people
passing away, as it's said—
disappearing almost unnoticed at the fringes
of the festivals of the young.
The young, who are us.

It will all live.
You will live
and for you to live
your earth will have to live
and it will live.

Where will you live
with your earth
and me still courting you?
Where will you live with your power
of the golden light
of a sunset that is the height
and centre of its day,

your power to look back
at our failure, yours and mine: your power
turning the lost world
to a rich and beautiful country
for walking through
forward into where?
I don't know. But you will live.

29–30 July 2016

APPENDICES TO PART V: ART OF SURGERY

APPENDIX 1
AUTHOR'S NOTE ON "ART OF SURGERY"

Although the poems of *As Far As You Know* have been kept in the order of composition, a different unity was added to the book and each section by selecting only certain poems of the ones from the years of composition. My idea was to combine poems to bring out themes while maintaining a diaristic form. The poems' order and their selection out of a larger group was to provide a picture of feeling and thought changing over a coherent period. This goes with my idea that the eternal moment is a moment with extension, including a before and after, and that the term "moment" indicates unity, not short (perhaps infinitely short) duration. The "now" has a before and after, a vital internal continuity. The sections were to show that an unbroken skein nonetheless contains defined moments.

A portion of such a unity of time is represented by the poems that cluster around "Art of Surgery" and take their group title from it. In one of its dimensions, this poem could be seen as opposing and balancing Blake's great "When old corruption first began," with its brusque, brutal, penetrating view of the origin, significance, and results of surgery, and of anatomy, on which modern surgery of course is based. Anatomy: the cutting up of the body to see how it works, leading us to the twofold and disastrous error that we can take an "objective" stance toward "our" body, viewing it as a something we possess. (But in fact we *are* "our" body, though not simply.) Correlative to this mistake, unavoidably growing from it, is the belief that our body is a machine to be worked on and repaired—an inferior, troublesome machine compared to thought-out and manufactured ones. This is an example, and an emblematic one, of scientific technology: it gives powerful results which justify themselves by their effectiveness and benefits, and it belittles human beings, removing grandeur and hope, other than that of surviving as long as possible, or rather, as long as viable. But an era which takes that for hope no longer has any hope and is itself a belittlement of the human.

In 2014, I was in hospital for about two weeks for a serious heart operation, and then for observation and the first part of my recuperation. "Art of Surgery" reflects this, but so do the other poems, or elements of them, sometimes obliquely. For instance, what I wanted to spend my time on, as soon as I was recuperating and was expected to walk around the hospital and sit in an atrium and so forth, was to read, and I read Vergil, the *Georgics*: hence "Vergil, Legend," although the poem wasn't written until later.

What I experienced in hospital was a very moving convergence of the human and the technical. Technique, both the bureaucratic organizational techniques and the scientific medical ones, absolutely compelled and constrained every worker I encountered. Each one had to work as a prescribed part of the system, had to work at set times, for set periods, at set tasks, according to set procedures. Even voice and mind were absorbed into the machine: the workers had to state set things; they had to give out forms and information sheets; and much of what they had to tell the patients or the families were scripts that they had to read or memorize. It was as if I were in the opposite situation of the oppressed industrial worker in Chaplin's satirical image in *Modern Times* of an assembly line. Rather than being the person who had to contribute one little identical twist to endless identical items coming past him on the conveyer, I was an inert stationary item under construction (or repair) and a dozen different workers had to be carried past me by the conveyer so they could each add their twist to me every day or every couple of days or every few hours.

Despite this, each one of them was human with me within the cubicle or cell of time that was all the system granted.

I could write, instead, that they tried with almost martyred determination and strain to be human with me, and that would be true and yet untrue. I could see that it was indeed hard for them to fit human togetherness into the methods and schedules that had to be served. But at the same time, and more basically, they naturally flowed toward this behaviour.

One could say that within the physically and organizationally remorseless environment, nature subsisted, as it does in our cities, partly nourished by our longing, and partly on its own just by bursting through the cracks or finding abandoned areas or shining down in the form of the sky that we can never annihilate. Or I could say, putting the same thing a different way, that the basic non-ideological anarchism of human beings, their tendency to submit all things to the free relationship of free persons, still struggled to be the governing factor, and had its victories, within the mandating system.

This factor—person-to-person reality—within the hospital system and the larger health care system, is even today never mentioned as its central factor and the only one preventing it from complete collapse into power and the absence of all human relevance. I say "even today" because, of course, under the almost-never-acknowledged-and-thanked impulse begun long ago by William Blake and Jacques Ellul and a few others, there has finally, in recent decades, begun to be a spreading awareness of the lack of human space in our systems and a chorus of calls for change. Yet these remain calls for fixes. Even the calls that present themselves as demanding radical transformation never yet envision what Ellul and Blake showed so clearly is necessary and right: the human person and interpersonal relationship at the base and centre, and technology only and always serving, strictly subordinated, and even eschewed when its use would unavoidably command rather than serve human behaviour.

Poetry, as Wordsworth teaches, is an action of creative response, of activity springing from wise passivity, action springing from and serving openness and afterwards returning to it. And so for me this experience in hospital was poetry and the germ of poetry. It was like a fresh revelation of my permanent sense of the heroism of people struggling simply to be people, fully, within the situations given to them, situations that often are needlessly tyrannical and restrictive and impoverishing but which still have to be used and have to be praised, because they let us live, they are our life, and life is good, we want to live. I wanted this rebirth or reinvigoration of faith in me to be permanent, a renewal permanent in itself and in each subsequent moment. I wanted this gratitude and admiration I felt to be permanent in my life.

This rebirth seemed to reach out and gather other feelings that have always obsessed me and give them added sharpness, the sense of invigoration and wide-seeing that comes with fresh clear air. Heroism: struggle for some good, usually quiet struggle in terrible circumstances. The ultimate depth of this: the praise of life despite the apparent equality of good and evil or even the predominance of evil: the praise that is true, because tested in both joyful and bitter experience and rising up as song: the praise named "beauty." The seemingly disparate themes of the poems in *As Far As You Know* seem to me all aspects of the same theme.

This, then, is what *As Far As You Know* and its subsections, such as "Art of Surgery," were to be about. I hear "to be about" not as meaning "to speak concerning" but "to do," in a way that subsumes the other sense, as the expression is used in "I must be about my father's business." I love Blake's critique of modern civilization and Ellul's critique of the "technological society." They are prophetic and exactly right about the world we live in. But I can dare to take an opposite view in part because these masters did so themselves, creating an intensely paradoxical or dialectical vision in which the human being is, at least so far, never destroyed, but preserves innocence and possibility, and even triumphs — if we can understand triumph not as power, wealth, prestige, prominence, technical effectiveness, if we can understand it truly, that is to say, poetically. As Juan Ramón Jiménez says in *Time and Space*, "Great is the small":

Grande es lo breve
y si queremos ser y parecer más grandes
unamos con amor.

"Great is what is brief and slight, and if we want to be and to seem greater, let us unite with love." It's not as if we do not know this, but we need—why do we always need?—to be reminded.

APPENDIX 2
THE POEM REFERRED TO IN "THE YEAR"

I should provide the poem that "The Year" references in its final stanza. This is "As I Understood It," which concluded my book *Here* (Portland, ME: Contraband Press, 1975). In the first edition of *Here* it had already been revised from its first magazine publication, and after that edition it's been published twice again with further revisions. But the changes are slight—minor rearrangements or rephrasing to clarify the interlace of hermetic symbols—and the present version is close to the wording and spirit of the first. I notice that in writing "The Year," I remembered the spaceship with a peach tree planted on its hull as representing the woman who is the subject of both poems, while in fact "As I Understood It" is ambiguous on this point but most strongly indicates the speaker of the poem, not the woman, as the one accused of having abandoned the earth.

As I Understood It

"As I understood it, living in the fountain,
the flower and fall of its angry rod
was destiny. And yet we had the power,
like a firework rocket that fails to burst,
to continue endlessly in imagination
for awaited stars. But water dropping back
ruffled the mirror, dispelling idle reflections
so no one was tempted to drown himself for love.

"This is the sense then of your independence
in the surrounding garden of arms that rise and fall,
chopping meat. The silver thread
I wanted around your hips was more beautiful

than your current business: yourself
going before you,
dropping parts of your body by the road.
While you were at meat, my mouth was full of silver.

"I had ascended into heaven,
vaguely, like water, only to be rudely dumped
on the plain way you snuffed the ground.
Now the peaches grow riper every day,
they ought to have fallen long ago,
and the too heavy brown spreads. I still want you
released from summer altogether,
like sunlight's colour that escapes the eyes."

This voice came back from a world of speculation
wrapped in the arms of a sister
to the lady whose ear it sought.
The peach tree planted on the stark sunlit
half of its hull, this ship drifts
in the black ocean of a starless night.

NOTES

epigraphs: "From the Rising of the Sun"; Czesław Miłosz, *New and Collected Poems 1931–2001* (Ecco/HarperCollins, 2001), 331. David V. Erdman, ed., William Blake, *The Complete Poetry and Prose of William Blake* (Doubleday, rev. ed. 1988), 141; from *Milton* plate 40 [46], lines 15–16.

page 7, "Terrorism": The quotation from Robinson Jeffers is from "Pearl Harbor"; Tim Hunt, ed., *The Collected Poetry of Robinson Jeffers* (Stanford University Press, 1991), vol. 3, 115–116.

page 8, "Terrorism": The phrase "The silver bird on high" is quoted from Gordon Lightfoot's song "Early Morning Rain."

page 35, "Baltimore May 2015": On 12 April 2015, Freddie Gray was arrested in Baltimore. During transport to the police station, Gray was sufficiently brutalized to break his neck and put him into a coma from which he never recovered. Protestors took to the streets on 18 April; Gray died the following day. Intensifying protests led to the declaration of a state of emergency and, on 1 May, the Baltimore medical examiner ruled Gray's death a homicide. The phrase "swift as arrow" is from William Blake, "The Blossom," *op. cit.* 7.

page 43, "The Twins": A story usually termed the myth of the hero twins is a central feature of Maya culture as reflected in the book *Popol Vuh*. It can be read in *Popol Vuh: A Sacred Book of the Maya, retold by Víctor Montejo*, tr. David Unger (Toronto: Groundwood Books, 1999, pbk. 2009). There is another good translation of *Popol Vuh* by Dennis

Tedlock. Traces of stories that resembled the Maya twins story are found elsewhere in Mesoamerica and in North America, for instance in the Mississippian (mound building) culture and the culture of peoples who inhabited what is now the state of Oklahoma.

page 54, "Sudden Little Parade Downtown": In the poem, the two snatches of Iroquoian (Seneca) and Maori poetry are followed by condensed paraphrases of their meanings in English. The Seneca lines appear in the transcription of *Songs from the Iroquois Longhouse*, William N. Fenton, Bureau of American Ethnology, the Archive of Folk Culture recording AFS L6. The lines are part of "Dream Song of Our Two Uncles, the Bigheads," which is a song for the stirring of ashes that is part of "the great festival of dreams at midwinter." The singer Joshua Billy Buck was quoted as rendering part of the song this way: "Now he has sung the dream song of our maker, who dwells in the sky, and now he has gone through the dream... Let all of us return thanks..." The Maori lines are exceedingly famous, since they are sung before test (international) matches by New Zealand's national rugby teams, the All Blacks and the Kiwis. They come from a haka composed very early in the nineteenth century by a war chief, Te Rauparaha, giving thanks for having escaped an enemy by hiding for the night in a dark hole. The stanza might be translated, "I may die, may die! I may live, may live! / I may die, may die! I may live, may live! / This is the well-haired man / who calls forth the sun and causes it to shine! / A step upward, another step! / A step upward, another step—the sun shines!"

page 74, "Our Dark Hands": The first four and a half lines of the fourth section are a paraphrase translation of lines from André Breton's "Sur la route de San Romano."

page 82, "Love, Thou Art Absolute Sole Lord": The title is from the opening of a poem by Richard Crashaw: "Love, thou art absolute sole lord / Of life and death." The phrase in quotation marks is a condensation of an aphorism of Victor Hugo as quoted by Octavio Paz in *The Other Voice: Essays on Modern Poetry*, trans. Helen Lane (Harcourt Brace Jovanovich, 1992), 159: "Hugo said it in a magnificent phrase: *Tout cherche tout, sans but, sans trêve, sans repos...*"

page 95, "The One Who Answers the Call": The poem's title is Jean Vanier's translation, occurring in more than one of his books, of the Greek scripture term "paraclete."

ACKNOWLEDGEMENTS

Some of the poems in *As Far As You Know* have been published in the journals *Audeamus, Literary Matters, Vallum, Volta,* and the *Yale Review*; in the books *A Throw of the Dice* (edited by Carleton Wilson; Junction Books Poem Pamphlet no. 1, 2016), *Tamaracks: Canadian Poetry for the Twenty-first Century* (edited by James Deahl; San Pedro, CA: Lummox Press, 2018), and *Art of Surgery* (edited by Eleni Zisimatos; Montreal: Vallum Chapbook Series no. 26, 2019); and on the website *Poetry Daily* ("Descent to the Dead", republished from *Vallum*). My thanks to the editors.

It's a pleasure to offer deep thanks to Michael Redhill, the substantive editor on this book as well as on my last, *The Sparrow: Selected Poems*, and to Kevin Connolly, poetry editor at House of Anansi, as well as to Sarah MacLachlan and all my friends at Anansi, my belovèd literary home.

Author photograph by Steve Payne

A. F. MORITZ is widely considered one of the defining and most beloved lyric poets of his generation. His many honours include a Guggenheim Fellowship, the Award in Literature from the American Academy and Institute of Arts and Letters, the Griffin Poetry Prize, the Bess Hokin Prize, and an Ingram Merrill Fellowship. He currently serves as the sixth poet laureate of the City of Toronto.